Diplôme

Le Bureau des Plus Belles Baies du Monde a reconnu que

PENGHU

est un site d'une beauté exceptionnelle et d'intérêt touristique majeur
et à ce titre, il a décidé de lui conférer

le titre de membre des PLUS BELLES BAIES DU MONDE

et autorise ses représentants à signaler cette distinction
sur tous les documents relatifs à la Baie.

Fait à **BERLIN**, le **7 Mars 2014**

Le Président   Le Secrétaire Général   Le Directeur
Galip Gür   Michel Bujold   Bruno Brébant

證書譯文 Certificate Translation

世界最美麗海灣組織在此認可：澎湖做為一個優美絕倫的觀光盛地，值得被賦予
「世界最美麗海灣」會員之名，在此准予澎湖於對外文件上註明此一榮譽。

The most beautiful bays in the world club affirms Penghu as an exceptional major
tourism desitination and it is worthy to be known as a member of "The most beautiful
bays in the world". The rights to use this honorable title is given to Penghu.

｜柏林世界旅遊博覽會授證｜

澎湖的美令人驚豔，躍居國際舞臺，深獲肯定。2013年「世界最美麗海灣」組織正式以「臺灣‧澎湖灣」名稱
通過入會申請。2014年在德國柏林世界旅遊博覽會授證，正式宣布澎湖成為「世界最美麗海灣」組織會員。

The Membership Certificate Of "The Most Beautiful Bays In The World"

The stunning beauty of Penghu has been recognized internationally. Penghu used title "Penghu Bay, Taiwan" and
applied to become a member of the organization: "The world's most beautiful bay" in 2013 and was accepted and
awarded the title in the 2014 the World Tourism Fair held in Berlin, Germany.

遙遠的1740萬年前，地層下躁動的岩漿在震盪中由裂縫噴發，臺灣海峽黑水溝湧出炙熱的玄武岩熔岩，幾經滄海桑田，留下如今澎湖多樣的島嶼奇景。大自然奇妙的力量，依著熔岩不同的噴發角度，經過地表的裂縫竄出，成就五角六角形的柱狀節理，成為澎湖豐富絢麗的玄武岩資源。

黑潮支流經過，孕育豐富海鮮水產，祖祖輩輩在這片土地上堅毅樂天生活，滋養出一方水土風情，生成菊島獨特人文風景。等你來乘風破浪，來細細體驗它的美麗與熱情。

17.4 Million years ago, the constant moving magma below the tectonic plates merged and created the basalt land now called Penghu. Through the ages, the wind and the sea shaped the island landscape. The basalt walls that were uniquely shaped by the magma, slowly reappeared by the cliffs. Its hexagonal shapes are the result of the magma's flow.

The passing of the black tide brings rich marine life and ocean resources, filling this island with prosperity. The unique marine resources forms unique ocean culture and local life style. This fantasy island is awaiting for you to explore.

目 錄

澎湖全島嶼地圖
The Map Of Penghu Islands

俄羅斯 Russia

蒙古 Mongolia

鄂霍次克海 Sea of Okhotsk

北韓 North Korea

日本海 Sea of Japan

南韓 South Korea

黃海 Yellow Sea

中國 China

日本 Japan

東海 East China Sea

尼泊爾 Nepal　不丹 Bhutan

孟加拉 Bangladesh

緬甸 Burma

印度 India

寮國 Laos

南海 South China Sea

菲律賓海 Philippine Sea

泰國 Thailand

越南 Vietnam

柬埔寨 Cambodia

安達曼海 Andaman Sea

菲律賓 Philippines

代夫海 adive Sea

斯里蘭卡 Sri Lanka

馬來西亞 Malaysia

Celebes Sea

印尼 Indonesia

澎湖 PENGHU

臺灣 TAIWAN

目斗嶼 Mudouyu

吉貝嶼 Jibeiyu

姑婆嶼 Gupoyu

白沙嶼 Baishayu

小門嶼 Hsiaomenyu

白沙鄉 Baisha Township

鳥嶼 Niaoyu

員貝嶼 Yuanbeiyu

雞善嶼 Gishayu

西嶼鄉 Hsiyu Township

大倉嶼 Datsangyu

錠鉤嶼 Dinggouyu

湖西鄉 Husi Township

四角嶼 Szjieuyu

查埔嶼 Chapuyu

雞籠嶼 Zilonyu

馬公市 Magong City

香爐嶼 Shiangluyu

查母嶼 Chamuyu

桶盤嶼 Tongpanyu

虎井嶼 Hujinyu

北回歸線 Tropic of Cancer　23.5°N

花嶼 Huayu

PENGHU
THE MOST BEAUTIFUL BAYS IN THE WORLD
ISLANDS

貓嶼 Mauyu

望安鄉 Wangan Township

將軍澳嶼 Jiangiyunyu

西吉嶼 Sijiyu

鋤頭嶼 Chutoyu

西嶼坪嶼 Siyupingyu

東嶼坪嶼 Dongyupingyu

東吉嶼 Donjiyu

七美鄉 Cimei Township

澎湖起飛　你我幸福　Let Us Share The Happiness And Let Penghu Soar

背起行囊，走進島嶼的海天一色，澎湖歡迎您。

澎湖是屹立於台灣海峽的小島，90多座大、小島嶼，綿延320多公里海岸線，自然景緻磅礡而渾然天成，世界級的壯麗玄武岩，是上帝灑落在海峽的珍珠，更是台灣唯一獲國際認證的「世界最美麗海灣」組織會員，天然美景與熱情島民融合出的海島風情，讓人流連難忘。

澎湖除了認證成為世界最美麗海灣，2015年分別入選亞洲新興旅遊城市、縣市首長滿意度全國第5、居民光榮感全國第1、居民幸福感全國第2。澎湖是臺灣最宜居的城市，也是最具國際觀光發展潛力的海島、旅遊天堂。

澎湖有陽光、沙灘、海浪、仙人掌，還有比臺灣本島早400年的開發史。旅遊在澎湖、文化在澎湖，澎湖的海島風情，一年四季正以不同姿態，等待您來探索、體驗，品味海的味道，一趟澎湖行，留下的將是滿滿幸福回憶。

茲以本書記錄澎湖一市五鄉的特色，將澎湖最迷人的風情一一呈現，跟世人分享這一份來自海島的驕傲，也歡迎您的蒞臨。

澎湖縣長　陳光復

Get your backpacks ready and see the island paradise, Penghu welcomes you.

Penghu is an island located in Taiwan Strait with 90 small islands surrounding it. With 320km of costal line, magnificent basalt rocks and wonderful landscape, Penghu is like a pearl placed by God in the middle of Taiwan Strait. As the only location in Taiwan certified as "The Most Beautiful Bays in The World", this island and the local islanders will leave you with unforgettable memories.

Besides being "The Most Beautiful Bays in The World", Penghu was nominated in 2015 as Asia's new best place for traveling. With the county governor's performance rated at national top 5, citizens' reported sense of hometown pride ranked first place, and citizen overall reported sense of happiness at national top 2, Penghu not only has the greatest potential for becoming a travel paradise, it is also the best city to live in.

The Sun, beach, waves, cactuses, and 400 years of history, Penghu is filled with culture and scenery. We hope you take some time off and explore the seasons of this island, because there are many sights for you to experience here. The food, culture, and passion of local residents will sure to leave you with lots of sweet memories.

This book showcases the various aspects, the charm and beauty of one city and five townships in Penghu. It also hopes to share the wonders of the islands. Welcome to Penghu.

Penghu County Governor **Guang-Fu Chen**

魅麗城市 美哉澎湖 Charm Of The City From The Beauty Of Penghu

　　澎湖縣近年來，就像田園裡的幼苗，歷經各級政府與社會各界的灌溉、施肥、除草、扶正、深耕下，日漸茁壯成長。春、夏、秋、冬一年四季，隨時隨地都可以目睹到歌詠澎湖生命的喜悅。從2011年獲得全球權威旅遊指南寂寞星球（Lonely Planet）評選為「10大秘密島嶼」的第7名、2012年再獲得「世界最美麗海灣」（The Most Beautiful Bays in the World）國際組織通過成為全球39個最美麗海灣之一。大家的努力與付出，不僅締造文化觀光與經濟產值的高度效益，也展現澎湖縣以小搏大的韌性與潛力，再一次證明澎湖縣有能力匯集全國焦點，躍升世界舞台。

　　菊島澎湖是個歷史悠久的海洋城市，藍天、碧海、沙灘、古厝、漁舟、海洋處處都蘊孕著許多人文薈萃，不論是歷史文化、田園風光、海洋景緻或社區活動，都能讓人感受到純樸、熱情、輕鬆與悠閒。實在值得各界一起來體驗這個魅「麗」城市，捕捉離島美不勝收的萬種風情。所以只要來一趟澎湖，將會讓你感受深刻的心底悸動。

　　如果有人問我，走訪那麼多的地方或國家，妳認為哪裡的風景最美麗？屆時，我將會毫不遲疑的回答說：「我的家鄉—澎湖」。即便我或許沒看過北極極光的奇幻，即便我或許沒見識過撒哈拉沙漠海市蜃樓，但是就算我見過、看過，我想，那也撼動不了澎湖在我心目中的美麗地位。因為不相信的話，正可翻閱欣賞本冊專輯，作為印證。

　　欣逢縣府編印澎湖家鄉美麗景緻專輯付梓之際，成為澎湖的共同歷史記憶，欣喜之餘，聊述數語，藉以分享地方璀燦之美，樂為之序。

澎湖縣議會議長　劉陳昭玲

Like a spring sprout receiving tender care, Penghu grows stronger everyday as it is cared by the government and community. All throughout the four seasons, people witness the happiness and liveliness of Penghu. Penghu is ranked the 7th on "Top 10 Secret Island" list from the international renowned tour guidebook "Lonely Planet" in 2011 and was listed as one of the 39 most beautiful beaches on earth by the international organization "The Most beautiful Bays in The World" by in 2012. All residebts' effort not only improves the tourist industry and the economy, but also proves Penghu's potential of shining on the international stage.

Ju-dao Penghu is an ocean paradise with blue skies, white sand beaches, historical buildings, fishing boats, and the island is filled with history, Old cultures of passion and simplicity are seen everywhere on the island such as the farms, fishing practices, and even local community events. This beautiful island is truly a place that needs to be explored; beauty that must be experienced. The moment you step on Penghu Island is the moment you have memories you will never forget.

If anyone ever asks me about which place that I've visited has the most beautiful scenery, no doubt I will answer "My hometown, Penghu". I've not seen the beauty of northern lights nor the mirage of Sahara, but even if I did, no other scenery can ever replace the beauty of Penghu in my heart. But don't just take my word for it, read through this book and see it for yourselves.

Penghu County Council Speaker Chao-Ling, Liu Chen

第一章 CHAPTER

美麗海灣 1

風與海的奇幻島嶼群

BEAUTIFUL BAY

Fantasy Islands Of The Wind And The Sea.

傳說，天上的星星投影到海面就變成澎湖
的群島，探索90座島嶼的行旅，讓我們一
同登上火山熔岩，見證風與海共創的奇幻
島嶼群，在這天與地之間，感受四時變幻
的不同體驗。

As the legend goes, the Penghu archipelago was formed
from the reflections of the stars high above on the surface
of the ocean. Let's explore the 90 islands shaped by the
magic from volcanoes, ocean and wind. The horizon
between the sky and the sea is where the stories begin.

23.5°的相遇／碧海玄武／心印菊島／海上明燈

The Meeting At N23.5 / Basaltic Sea / Love For Penghu / Sea Light

美麗的嵵裡沙灘 │ The Beauty Of ShiLi Beach　N235253138, E119°5681948

| 北寮赤嶼分海奇景 |

退潮時，裸露出S型步道，蜿蜒至赤嶼，
站在岸邊觀賞彷彿是摩西分海合海的奇景。

N23.5627946, E119.6405398

澎湖
新十景
PENGHU
New 10 scenery

Beiliao Kui-Bi Mountain

A S-shaped trail occurs only during the low tide. Many say that this sight resembles the ancient story of Moses parting the Red sea.

| 菓葉日出 | 『菓葉日出』是澎湖古八景之一。晨曦乍現，海面上迸射萬道金色光芒，一輪火球浴海而出，抖落滿天雲彩，隱約中可望見臺灣中央山脈的輪廓。　N23.5781419, E119.6796792

GuoYe Sunrise　　The "GuoYe Sunrise" is one of the eight sights not to be missed in Penghu. On a good and clear day, you may even be able to see the outline of Taiwan's Central Mountain Range.

石滬落霞 │ Sunset On Stone Weir N23.625699, E119.503790 **023**

碧海玄武

在時間洪流的彼端，遼闊湛藍的海洋太寂寞，我們永恆的母親-地球從海底伸出她的手指，形成航行船隻、往返候鳥、親潮與黑潮交會的魚群，休息、繁衍、補給的澎湖山。

It is a place for birds and the fish to call home, a place where fishermen can rest on shore, truly a paradise.

大池角玄武岩石柱 | Basalt Walls In DaChiJiao　　N23.509676, E119.514922

澎湖 新十景
PENGHU
New 10 Scenery

| 桶盤玄武岩之美 |　柱狀玄武岩的島嶼奇景，有澎湖黃石公園之稱，其中以宛如蓮花座的海底火山口的海蝕平臺最為奇觀。　N23.509676, E119.514922

TongPan Basalt Walls　The wonders of basalt columns are results of volcano eruption tens of thousands years ago. Some say it is the Yellowstone Park of Penghu.

仙人掌冰淇淋 | Cactus Apple Ice Cream

仙人掌果 | Cactus Fruits.

| 崖邊的仙人掌 | 本地居民將野生仙人掌果實製成仙人掌冰及果汁，受到觀光客喜愛，食品加工業者也推出仙人掌果凍、仙人掌果醬及仙人掌酒等產品。

Cactuses By The Cliff   Local residents harvest wild cactus fruits, many of which grow on dangerous cliffs by the ocean.. These cactus fruit are then made into different products such as cactus ice and juice. There are many other products that are created from the fruits, such as wine, jelly, and jam. They have become quite popular among tourists.

海上明燈 GUIDING LIGHT ON THE CAST OCEAN

澎湖列島星羅棋布，大小島嶼近百，臺灣海峽黑水溝處處暗礁，海上燈塔默默屹立，指引漁家船舶平安歸來。

Penghu islands consist of hundreds of small islands; there are reefs and ditches everywhere. It is very dangerous to sail during the night, and the lighthouses serve as guardians, leading and guiding the sailors to safety.

臺澎地區最古老的燈塔，也是國家二級古蹟。光緒元年1875年建造，塔高3丈8尺，造型為圓柱狀，鐵造塔身為白色。

N23.562595, E119.468527

Fishermen's Island Lighthouse

The oldest lighthouse inTaiwan, it is also a Class 2 historic site. It was built in 1875, standing at 12.7 meters with cylindrically shaped white walls.

← | 目斗嶼燈塔 |

1899（明治32）年創建，燈塔塔高39.9公尺，塔身漆以黑白相間的橫條紋，為臺灣塔身最高的燈塔，是遠東最高的銑鐵製燈塔 N23.7862892, E119.6004414

MuDou Island Lighthouse

Built in 1899, the lighthouse is 39.9 meter tall. Painted with black and white horizontal stripes, this is the tallest lighthouse in Taiwan and the tallest lighthouse made of iron in the far eastern region.

| 漁翁島燈塔的幸福郵筒 |
Fishermen's Island Postal Box

花嶼燈塔

為澎湖群島中唯一玢岩地質島嶼。島上奇石遍佈，構成天然景觀，島嶼西南方是豐富漁場，夜晚時分漁火點點，景觀奇特。　　N23.402706, E119.316286

Huayu Island Lighthouse

Within the Penghu archipelago, Huayu island have the most unique rock formations. It is also the geologically oldest island, filled with unique stones. The lights from the nearby fishing boats are a spectacular sight.

東吉燈塔

自古即為臺澎海運貿易的轉運站，曾經繁華一時。從北方的山頭俯眺，紅瓦白牆的古厝襯托著青草及羊群，景色怡人。　N23.226549, E119.6913766

DongJi Island Lighthouse

Once an prosperous island, Penghu was a major stop for trades. Looking down from the hill top on the north side of the island, a delightful sight with heads of goats and traditional housing.

第二章 CHAPTER

人文歷史 2

笙歌漁歌 海島時光足跡

TRADITIONS & HISTORY

Songs Of Tales, Stories Of The Past.

澎湖群島，是臺灣海峽中最大的島礁群，海洋資源豐富，足以長久居住、子孫綿延、薪火相傳。歷史洪流中，有人路過、有人駐留、有人生產、有人掠奪，從衝突到戰爭，澎湖群島是臺灣海峽中最重要的軍事據點。真心祈禱，戰火在藍色海洋中永遠熄滅，這些古堡永不再點燃火砲。

Penghu archipelago is the largest island group in the Taiwan Strait. It is full of marine resources, a place to settle and to prosper. Over the past hundreds of years, some people came to visit, some came to stay, and some came to conquer. Penghu also witnessed its fair shore of conflicts because of it has been an important strategic location for military action. The remains of military structures such as forts were evidence of such past. We certainly wish those old forts will never be put to use again.

守護菊島／舊昔今觀／心誠則靈／西瀛風情

Long Live Penghu / View Of The Past / Prayers / XiYing Life Style

失落的地平線……東嶼坪遠眺西嶼坪 | Lost In The Horizon, A View Of XiYuPing Island For DongYuPing Island.

N23.259378, E119.514836

守護菊島 LONG LIVES PENGHU

風、海與陽光的島嶼，美麗菊島，萬縷風情中帶著神祕，始終吸引無數愛慕者前去與她
邂逅，談一場戀愛。

她雖在歷史戰火中走過、帶著些許傷痕，但這些未曾減弱陽光的灑落、減損富饒的海
洋，更不曾撼動風的子民想打造一個兼具風土與生活內涵之富庶島嶼的決心。

Wind, ocean and sun are just a regular part of Penghu Life. The island is lovely and mysterious
at times. She's also scarred from her past. However, the turbulent past never shakes the
residents' determination to build a beautiful island, Penghu. She is filled with mystery where
many are attracted to understand her, to love her.

媽宮城

建於1887年（光緒十三年），用以提昇澎湖的防衛能力，當時設有六座城門。如今僅剩下順承門和大西門（今中興門）見證媽宮城的歷史，是頗受歡迎的旅遊景點。

N23.562955, E119.562632

Magong City

The old walls were built for defense purposes in 1887 during the time of war. There were originally 6 walls in total, but only two: ShunCheng Gate and DaXi Gate survived and remained. These two gates are popular tourist attractions now.

← 蛇頭山陣亡將士紀念碑

蛇頭山位於馬公風櫃尾北端突出的小半島上，與北岸的金龍頭共同扼守馬公灣，形勢險要，遠眺馬公港測天島及四角嶼等澎湖內灣。此地為當年法軍侵澎登陸地，據文獻記載，1622年荷蘭人曾建有一座最早的荷蘭城堡。　N23.55164, E119.547565

SheTou Mountain Monument

SheTou Mountain is located at the north end of FengGui. Together with the north shore JinLongTou, CeTian island, and SiJiaoYu, they formed the major defense line against invading French army. In 1622 the Dutch built a fort right on SheTou Mountain.

西嶼西臺古堡

清代劉銘傳於1887年(光緒十三年)所督建的西式砲臺，
以作為軍事海防之用。此堡壘也是清廷水師的基地。
N23.5640739, E119.4892859

XiYu West Fort
The XiYu Western Fort was built in 1887 when Lou Ming
Chuang from the Qin dynasty was in charge of defending
the island from pirates.

西臺

| 仿阿姆斯壯後膛砲 | Armstrong Cannon

| 西嶼東臺內部設施 | Inside Xiyu Eastern Fort

與西嶼西臺為同期興築的砲臺，內有圓拱形磁磚構造的兵房及彈藥庫圓拱形磚石構造的，與馬公金龜頭砲臺共同扼守媽宮港。現與西嶼西堡壘、東堡壘，東昌營區共同規劃成西嶼東臺軍事史蹟園區。　　N23.5656223, E119.5118592

XiYu Eastern Fort

The Eastern Fort was built in the similar fashion around the same time. Inside the fort are rooms for soldiers and armory. These two forts and the Dong Cheng Camp are now part of the historical military park.

| 澎湖蒙面女郎 |

風大沙多，蒙面女郎是適應澎湖特殊天候條件而來，是澎湖地區婦女的特有穿著衣飾。

Penghu's Masked Women

The gusty wind brings dusts. These masked women are examples of local residents' adaptation to the windy weather condition.

| 西嶼牧情 |

夕陽西下，牛兒看到主人，喊著要帶牠回家，興奮地撒嬌。

Herding Cattle In Xiyu

As the Sun sets, the ox is happy to go home with its owner.

| 外垵漁港 | 美麗的垵澳一面臨海，三面皆有高丘做為屏障，房舍依地勢而建，藍與白交織，充滿慵懶悠閒的海洋氣息，日與夜的西嶼都是最美的景緻。　N23.5638885, E119.4805556 |

WeiAn Harbour　Facing the ocean and surrounded by the hills, the houses are builts alog the hills and create an interesting view of the local community. The relaxing atmosphere of the beach is everywhere in the village. Siyu is beautiful regardless time of the day.

| 漁港補網 |

捕魚空檔來補網⋯⋯也編織一份期待滿載的心情。

Mending Fishing Nets, A Typical Sight At Fishing Harbors
Mending fishing nets when not working on the boat.

| 虎井嶼 |

島上中央低平，東西兩端為突起台地，柱狀節理玄武岩排列於險峻海崖邊，仰望氣勢雄偉，東山海底有一狀似城牆之遺址，即昔日澎湖八景之一「虎井澄淵」。　N23.486659, E119.516427

HuJing Islet

HuJing island is known for its geological treasure. Under the east ocean lies an ancient wall thought to be a part of old city structure. This is one of the eight sights to visit in Penghu.

| 漁港之晨 | 漁船靠岸漁工忙著拋纜。 N23.5654576, E119.5692428

Dawn At The Harbor　Fisherman on the boat tossing ropes.

西瀛夕照釣魚趣

趁著夕陽西下霞光漫漫，三五好友相聚岸邊垂釣，這可是島民午後最大的樂趣。

Fishing During Sunset

Fishing with friends and enjoying the lovely sunset is the favorite pastime of the locals.

第三章 CHAPTER

經濟營生
海洋故鄉生養樂天鄉民

3

MAKING A LIVING
Co-living With Ocean And Content Residents.

澎湖人，位於北緯23.5°海角一端踏實築夢的人，生活簡單樸實，無懼於臺灣海峽冬季東北季風極端氣候環境，憑著一股傻勁，實在認命過日子，創造獨特的經濟生活方式，歡喜營生。他們順天而為的樂天個性，不僅活出精采，也為這世界最美麗海灣增添了不凡的美麗色彩。

Penghu people are those who built their own dreamland despite all the challenges from the natural environment. Live a simple lifestyle without any fears from the harsh strong northern winds. Some may think this is foolish, but this allowed Penghu people to create a unique way of life of cope with the environment. Their easy going attitude makes the mood of the island more exciting, creating an even better island lifestyle.

以海為生／人與土地／世代傳藝

Living With The Sea / People And Land / Passing Of Traditions

外垵漁港 | WeiAn Harbur　N23.5638885, E119.4805556

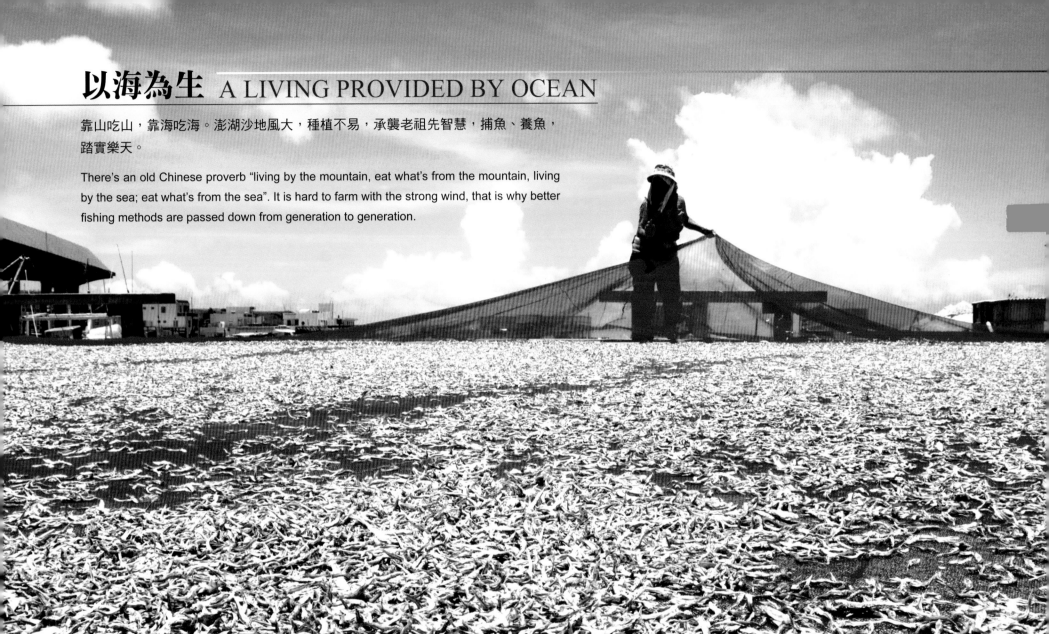

以海為生 A LIVING PROVIDED BY OCEAN

靠山吃山，靠海吃海。澎湖沙地風大，種植不易，承襲老祖先智慧，捕魚、養魚，踏實樂天。

There's an old Chinese proverb "living by the mountain, eat what's from the mountain, living by the sea; eat what's from the sea". It is hard to farm with the strong wind, that is why better fishing methods are passed down from generation to generation.

船上煮丁香魚 | Cooking Slender Sprats On A Fishing Boat　N23.666432, E119.603879

揀 魚 | Fish Picking

赤崁漁港是白沙鄉最重要的捕丁香魚漁港，澎湖大部分的丁香魚都是在此海域捕撈，每年4至9月是丁香魚產期。

ChiKan harbor is the major part of BaiSa village for slender sprat fishing. Most of the slender sprats are fished from here during months of April to September.

丁香魚灶 | Furnace For Cooking Slender Sprat

| 潛水捕捞 | 漁人潛水撿拾海膽或水中貝類等物。

Dive Gathering Fishermen dive to pick up sea urchins and clams.

| 夕陽漁翁 | Fisherman And The Sunset

| 潮間帶剌蛤仔 | Gathering Calms In Intertidal Zon

澎湖群島的潮間帶資源豐富，漁村婦女趁退潮時撿拾螺貝。夜晚時分魚蝦螃蟹都出來
覓食，村民在大退潮的夜晚會攜帶燈具到潮間帶捕捉這些海味，俗稱「照海」。

Due to Penghu's unique landscape, there are many intertidal zones throughout the
island. Many villagers,especially women tread on the intertidal zones to pick fish, crabs
and shrimps when they come out to feed during low tide in the evening. The light from
villagers' lanterns light up the beach and the, locals call this "ChouHai" (light on ocean).

｜外垵漁火｜

夜間萬點漁火流動，忽明忽滅，照映水中宛如落凡星斗，1953年「澎湖漁火」選定為臺灣八景之一。

N23.564429, E119.480835

WeiAn Flaming Boats

On the Lantern Festival, all the fishing boats in the harbor turn on lights, creating a fantastic view. The local calls this "Penghu flaming boats". In 1953, this celebration was chosen as one of the eight must-see sight in Taiwan.

｜豐收時刻｜ 清晨漁船捕魚收網，海鳥也會圍繞著搶食新鮮的海味。

Bountiful When fishing boats cast nets early in the morning, seagulls want a share of catch.

｜澎湖一支釣｜

手持釣竿戲弄魚蝦，耳聞浪濤拍岸吼聲，別是新鮮刺激樂趣橫生。

Fishing in Penghu

Fishing and listening to the roaring sea is all the fun and excitement.

| 曬小管 | Squid Drying

夏天是澎湖燈火漁業捕撈洄游性魚類的漁汛期，在地人會把丁香、扁魚、四破、象魚、臭肉等魚類簡單鹽煮後，曬成魚乾後延長保存期限，一年四季都可食用。

Spot light fishing is a common fishing method used to catchmigratory fishes that come to Penghu during summer time. These fish are salted, dehydrated and preserved for other seasons.

| 曬鮇鉅 |

鮇鉅燉排骨加螺肉，澎湖傳統美食

Octopus Drying

Octopus cooked with ribs, a traditional delicacy.

| 井垵曬魚場 | Fish-Drying Square　N23.518762, E119.576504

| 曬魚干 | Preserving Fish

| 正庄古早味……去骨曝豆油糖臭肉乾 |

臭肉魚去骨後，浸泡豆油、糖、蒜頭，再灑上芝麻曬乾
烤來吃香味四溢，口齒留香，近來已很少有這味了。

A True Traditional Cuisine: Dry Fish Fillet In Soy Sauce And Sugar

Filleted Japanese gizzard shads are hung up to dry after being marinated in soy sauce,
sugar, garlic, and then sprinkled with sesame seeds. This is a rare delicacy these days.

| 石斑魚養殖 | 澎湖海域海水清淨，運用海水潮汐養殖法，讓石斑魚肉質鮮美，在海鮮市場上贏得好名聲！

Farm-Raised Groupers　The high quality of sea water allows excellent aquaculture industry which high-quality groupers.

姑婆嶼挽紫菜

既神秘又充滿傳說的島嶼，也是北海面積最大的無人島，
北岸的海蝕平臺因長年受到浪濤覆淋，是著名的天然紫菜產地。
N23.520393, E119.573472

Seaweed On Gupo Island

Gupo Island is mysterious and filled with legends. It is
also the largest uninhabited island in the northern part of
Penghu. Its rocky beaches are ideal place to grow seaweed.

潮間帶海菜

春寒料峭的潮間帶海域，彷若打翻一片碧綠墨水，隨浪擺動
如跳曼波水舞，青青海菜正述說著一頁海田傳奇。

Seaweeds On Intertidal Zone

Waves of Seaweed on the intertidal zone.

第一酒廠

以澎湖獨特農產植物，開發仙人掌酒、風茹酒、蘆薈酒、金瓜酒等養生酒類，以提高一般農民收入，並建立高產值精緻農產。

N23.569105, E119.5949055

The First Brewery

Cactus wine, Glossogyne tenuifolia tea, aloe wine, and pumpkin wine are all specialty products made from Penghu's local produce. These high-value products significantly increase farmers' income.

美酒處處飄香 | The Aroma Of Wine

喝酒不開車、飲酒勿過量
Please drink responsibly

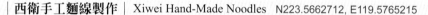

池東屋頂曬麵線 | Noodles Being Processed On Roof Top In Chidon N23.5972014, E119.5059384　　西衛手工麵線製作 | Xiwei Hand-Made Noodles N223.5662712, E119.5765215

第四章 CHAPTER 4

島嶼旅遊

多元體驗 海上樂土

ISLAND PARADISE

A paradise with endless fun.

讓世界看見澎湖，這一座渾然天成、文明便利的海上樂土，匯集地質、水文、氣候、地理位置等優勢條件，這裡有最豐富的海洋生態、最多元的水上活動，甚至可體驗如摩西神蹟般，分開海洋，走過海底的寶貴時刻。自然與文明共存，安全與便利同在，整串島列像珍珠一般撒在海上、張開雙臂，歡迎每一個訪客的到來。

So many way to experience the beauty of this ocean paradise. The combination of rich marine life, geological landscape, mild weather and location provide the perfect environment for visitors to experience true Penghu island life. The coexistence of nature and civilization creates a safe and convenient island that welcomes all visitors with open arms.

樂活一夏／菊島映像／快樂行腳／菊島之光

Summer Fun Time / Island Imagery / Happy Trails / Glory Of Penghu

美麗的島嶼：吉貝嶼和險礁嶼 | Beautiful Islands, JiBei And XianJiao Island.

樂活一夏 SUMMER FUN TIME

湛藍的海、金黃的沙、白色的浪，海底熱帶魚及珊瑚群相當豐富，是浮潛、戲水的天堂。你可以恣意的在沙灘上享受日光浴、堆沙、沙灘排球……等活動，好不愜意。

Blue sky, golden sand, white waves, diverse marine life, and beautiful reefs, this is a paradise for snorkeling and swimming. You can enjoy sunbathing on the beach, building sand castles, playing beach volleyball, and many more activities.

│隘門沙灘│ Aimen Beach N23.5548761, E119.6368896

| 香蕉船 | Banana Boat

| 衝浪板 | Surf Board

| 水上摩托車 | Jet Ski

澎湖是水上活動的天堂，香蕉船、滑水漢堡、拖曳圈、衝浪飛毯、水上摩托車等多樣豐富刺激的水上活動，保證讓玩家們驚叫連連。

Penghu is the best location for any water sports such as banana boats, surfing burgers, surfing discs, surfing carpets, and jet skis. All of them are stimulating and exciting. Fun is guaranteed.

赤馬沙灘 | Chima Beach   N23.58645, E119.5021812

| 山水沙灘 | ShanShui Beach   N23.5129764, E119.5888912

澎湖跨海大橋西嶼端
主要聯繫白沙和西嶼之間，是西嶼地區重要的交通命脈，長度為2600公尺，也是臺澎最長的橋。

View of Penghu's Sea Bridge From Xiyu
This bridge is the most important connection between Baisa and Xiyu. Wit a total length of 2,600m, it is the longest bridge in Taiwan.

澎湖跨海大橋白沙端
View Of Penghu's Sea Bridge From Baisa
N23.6511606, E119.5463582

南海遊客服務中心 | Southern Coast Visitor's Center

南海之星1號 | Nanhaixishin 1

| 南海碼頭 |

前往七美、望安、虎井、桶盤或其他南海小島，都由南海碼頭出發，每日上午七點到九點以及下午三點到五點，是快艇出航與返航的尖峰時間，碼頭上熱鬧非凡。　N23.5663398, E119.5726711

Southern Harbor　The southern coast visitor's center is where the boats to Chimei, Wanan, Hujing, and Tongpan are. The rush hour for speed boat traffic is from 7:00AM to 9:00AM and 3:00PM to 5:00PM.

南寮站 幸福巴士 | Nanliao BusStation

臺華輪 |

是航行於高雄－馬公之間的豪華客輪，總噸位8134噸，航速22浬，載客量1150人，載車能量小客車約100部（可兼載高層大客車、大貨車）。

N23.562681, E119.563381

Taihua Vessel

Weighting in 8134 tons, speed at 22 nodes, and max capacity at 1,150 passengers and 100 cars, this is the boat that travels between Kaohsiung and Magong.

南海之星2號 | 耗資2.4億元全新打造的「南海之星2號」客貨交通船，為馬公到望安、七美兩島間的交通運輸，提供更舒適、安全、快速的服務。　N23.649897, E119.6043006

Nanhaixishin 2 | It cost 240 million TWD to build the brand new Nanhaixishin 2. This vessel is a vital transport method that provides a safe and fast ride to southern islands.

菊島之光 GLORY OF PENGHU

澎湖島民有七百年的歷史，大海洋流黑潮與親潮更在此交會，交織出各式各樣的故事，才更覺得澎湖美麗的大自然，有著耀眼的光芒。

From seven centuries ago, there are already people living on Penghu. The tides joint together here and weaved many stories of the past; these stories show the natural beauty of Penghu and the glory of Penghu.

| 風箏浪板 | 強勁的東北季風及島嶼密佈，被國際風浪板組織列為世界排名前十大風浪板比賽場地。夏天水溫舒適，海水清澈，風力也非常適合初學者的體驗及教學風浪板競速。 |

Kite Surfing   The strong northern wind of winter attracts many sail surfers to come and compete in races. Penghu is recognized as the one of the top 10 sail surfing locations in the world. Summer season is the perfect time for beginners to learn sail surfing.

108

澎湖海峽杯帆船錦標賽

無數的神秘島嶼以及金色沙灘，吸引我們登上美麗帆船滑出港口，合力揚起船帆，一起從澎湖灣出發，開始美麗的旅程。

Penghu Sail Boat Race

The many islands and golden beaches of Penghu are attracting us to set sail and to explore. Starting from Penghu, let the adventure begin.

| 講美少棒 | 澎湖講美少棒隊以一所不到60人的迷你離島小學之姿，勇奪2002年亞洲少棒錦標賽冠軍，再度打造了離島棒球少棒隊的不朽傳說！ N23.6323624, E119.5966644

Jiangmei Junior Baseball Team   Jiangmei junior baseball team is from a small elementary school the has only 60 students, but they were able to win the Asia junior baseball league championship in 2002. This is an honor of Penghu that will go on for ages.

111

澎湖國際海上花火節

澎湖縣最負盛名的年度活動，每年吸引許多國內外遊客參與盛會，在雅虎奇摩網站上榮獲最受網友青睞的全國節慶活動第二名，僅次於同年舉辦的臺北國際花卉博覽會。澎湖花火節也入選2013年交通部觀光局舉辦的「臺灣觀光年曆縣市國際活動」，在國內外均累積高知名度。

Penghu International Firework Festival

Penghu firework show is the event that you don't want to miss. Every year thousands of people from over the world come to watch the sky lit up in bright colors. The event was voted the top 2 event to go to according to the search engine Yahoo, a runner-up to the International Botanical show in Taipei. The firework show is also listed as the one of the most well-known events in Taiwan by Taiwan Tourism Bureau.

西瀛虹橋亮點 | 彩虹橋為馬公的夜晚增添更多美麗的色彩。 N23.5694106, E119.5598799

Rainbow Bridge The rainbow bridge bring more colors to the nights of Magong city.

第五章 CHAPTER 5
永續生活
當我們平衡共存
SUSTAINABLE LIVING
Coexisting In Harmony

生存最大的智慧，就是「永續」。千萬年來，綠蠵龜還是上岸產卵、燕鷗也不想遷移到別處去，這裡不僅僅是人類的樂土，更是數千、數萬種生命的快樂天堂。如果你以為無線網路、衛星涵蓋、自動化機器，就能代表「智慧國土」，那麼你應該到澎湖來，體驗一下大自然的智慧－永續的平衡，才是最高的智慧。

The key to survival is sustainability. For millions of years, green turtles still return to nest to lay eggs, wild birds never move to other islands. This paradise not only belongs to humans alone, but is shared amongst all creatures. If you think wireless internet, satellite coverage, and automatic machinery represent a land is wisdom, then you are missing out the wisdoms of nature. Here in Penghu nature and technology coexist, creating a sustainable balance, this is the true wisdom.

生態保育／低碳島嶼

Ecological Conservation / Low-Carbon Island

| 雞善嶼 | 島嶼四周柱狀玄武岩，外型高低變化多端，宛如管風琴之琴管環繞。 N23.626618, E119.685821

Jishan Island Island is surrounded by basaltic walls in a variety of shapes and sizes, resembling pipe organs.

生態保育 ECOLOGICAL CONSERVATION

飛鳥與魚，大自然孕育的豐沛生命力。

3萬5千公頃的珊瑚礁群，化成美麗的澎湖海灣。玄武岩地質的壯闊奇崖，少有人工鑿痕的秀麗海岸，構成世界最美麗的海灘，有綠蠵龜迴游產卵。北方冷流和南方黑潮交會下的豐饒海洋資源，有天人菊、仙人掌映著湛藍海岸線。

Wild birds and fish are the living force of nature.

35,000 hectare of reefs, great basaltic walls, and very few man-made structures are just some of the reasons why Penghu is stunningly beautiful. Every year green turtles return to beach to lay eggs. Every winter the black tides collide with the northern streams and create a rich marine ecosystem. Tianranju and cactuses create a beautiful horizon along the shorelines.

| 鳳頭燕鷗 | Crested Terns

| 探索燕鷗 | 每當候鳥遷徙季節時，澎湖群島成為賞鳥者夏季觀賞燕鷗的天堂。夏季以燕鷗家族為最大，常見的種類有紅燕鷗、蒼燕鷗、小燕鷗、白眉燕鷗、玄燕鷗與鳳頭燕鷗6種。澎湖縣政府於民國81年公告縣內無人島小白沙嶼、雞善嶼及錠鉤嶼為禁止登岸的玄武岩自然保留區，貓嶼為全臺第一處海鳥保護區。

Discovering Terns   During the migration season, varieties of wild bird travel to Penghu. Many bird-watchers come to Penghu just to experience these wonderful creatures. Wild birds from the sterna family mostly visit during the summer. The most common species are roseate tern, black-naped tern, tern, bridled tern, brown noddy, and crested terns. In 1992, the county government officially named Xiaobaisa island, Jisan island, and Dinggou island a natural basalt landscape reserve area. Visiting the island is now prohibited.   Maoyu Island is the first designated wild birds' reserve area.

澎湖縣鳥
PENGHU COUNTY BIRD

| 小雲雀 | Oriental Lark

| 魚飛滿天　燕鷗追獵 | Seagull Hunting Flying Fish

| 青螺溼地紅樹林保育區 |

青螺村擁有廣大的濕地，春秋過境的水鳥常來覓食，村廟前的紅樹林，是澎湖最大的紅樹林保育區。

Lo Green Lin Baoyu Mangrove Wetland Area

Many wild birds visit Chinluo village's wetlands to feast during autumn and spring seasons.
The mangrove in front of the village temple is the largest mangrove reserve area.

黑面琵鷺也來澎湖過冬
Black-Faced Spoonbill Visiting Penghu During Winter

愛吃螃蟹的中杓鷸 | Whimbrel Loves To Eat Carbs

水鳥過境 | Spot-Billed Duck Passing By

119